Larn Y

by

Scott Dobson

BUTLER PUBLISHING
Thropton, Rothbury NE65 7LP

First published by Frank Graham

INTRODUCTION

This book has been written with the intention of making you a fluent speaker of Geordie. It is many years since I first perceived the need for such a book – in fact I was a schoolboy at the time. I attended a local institution of education and was, I recall, greatly upset by a dreadful act of revionism when a master was appointed to teach us 'speech'. He insisted that such words as the ancient and beautifully mellifluous 'clarts' should no longer be used. Instead we should say 'mud', or rather 'mahd'. I am happy to report that within six months he broke and was subsequently drummed out of the National Union of Teachers and blackballed at the Lit. and Phil.

I think it was because the moment of crisis came one morning at religious assembly when he prefaced the introductory prayer by beaming at us over his bifocals and saying – "What fettle the day, lads? – Eyes doon – luk in".

I hope you won't mind me giving a little of the historical background of the Geordie language. I feel that it is necessary because Geordie is *not*, repeat *not*, a regional accent. It is a language in its own right. Admittedly it owes much to Scandinavian tongues, for the Geordies and the Vikings had much in common, and still have. Both races were always very keen on chatting up each others birds and burning down monasteries. The Vikings actually made a League in monastery-burning and it became a major sport. The Geordies used to have a whip round and charter a flight to Oslo for the return matches. Unfortunately, these matches, both home and away, were stopped in 1537 by King Henry VIII of England who, in between honeymoons, had decided to suppress the monasteries. Having acquired a controlling interest in Tottenham Hotspur he wished to promote football instead, besides which he thought monastery-burning was getting too much of a sissy game and wished to re-establish a good clean sport like Soccer.

Talking about Hotspur reminds me that I have a duty to demolish a most untruthful legend about the Geordie language. The Percy family of Northumberland were a very rough lot of lads. They had to be in those days with a name like Percy. One of these Percys, Harry Hotspur, got the credit of introducing into the language the Geordie 'R' sound. This was just not so. Although they said that the Geordies copied his 'R' it was really the other way about. Seeing that his father had put his name down for Eton, he had to go to public school like the rest of the barons. However, when he came back to the North he found he couldn't even get served in the Alnwick Bannockburn Memorial Comrades Club. They didn't know what he was talking about. Having acquired a taste for federation beer while visiting the Houses of Parliament there was only one thing to do. He went to Rutherford College so that he could speak like everybody else. You might as well know, too, just how the tale got about that Hotspur invented the Geordie 'R'. With all the native cunning of successful coal-owners the Percys sent down south for a script-writer called

Couldn't get served in the Alnwick club!

William Shakespeare who, having served his apprenticeship on "Coronation Street" and "Close the Coalhouse Door" was doing rather well in the West End. For the fee of 10,000 ducats and free coal he agreed to write Harry into a part for his next show – "Henry IV".

This had its première at the Memorial Theatre, Stratford on Avon, which was run by Shakespeare's brother Fred, and did a further tour at the Newcastle Playhouse and the People's Theatre. You may have seen it advertised and reviewed in the Newcastle Evening Chronicle. The reviewer, who was Shakespeare's sister Agnes, called it "a most promising effort by a new playright which had the customers in a continual chuckle". Harry got a Life Peerage, a seat on the Coal Board and an Hon. M.A. from Newcastle University for his contribution to the Geordie language. I'm not making any accusations but you can look up the name of the University Chancellor if you like. Worse revelations are yet to come. Have you noticed how the Geordie language is musical?

How it goes up and down? When a Geordie speaks on any subject it sounds like the opening part of a Pontifical High Mass or Ravi Shankar singing Indian pops. It *sounds like music*. The pop music business has noticed this. Do you know that all the top groups are getting material for their new records from the Geordie language? Of course you don't – it has been suppressed by the popular musical press. Secretly they have been visiting Geordie-land for years with a tape recorder. Their method is simple. They visit working men's clubs in the area, start a controversy and locking themselves in the gents netty they record the resulting tumult through the keyhole. When all's quiet they nip out and within twenty-four hours that melodic Geordie string of curses is orchestrated in London and given a lyric by Noel Coward (they keep that quiet too). Evidence? I have here on my desk the transcript of a telephone call from my old friend Sam Slagheap, chairman of the Busty Pit Club Philosophical Society. You may read it literally in his own melodic brogue: Whey there's tnis group cums inter wor club caallin' thursels "The Skitters". Whey aad Tom on the door lets them in thinkin' they wez

up for the Go-as-you-please. Whey the' starts workin' themselves, man, the languidge was aaful. The' wez tappin' up the barmaids, one tried te date the chairman and the' wez tryin' te flog aal these pornographic undergroond byeuks. (Whey the' wez ne good tiv us cos wor club hasn't got a pornograph.) Then the' starts on aboot hoo useless Lord Robens wez, hoo the' wished Harold Macmillan wez back and by the time the'd got on te detonators in the coal and hoo the' were thinkin' aboot puttin' in oil heatin' at hyem the lads wez ready te massacree them. Me and the concert secretary wez shootin' – "Let's hev the best of order" but it wez ne gud–there wez hell on. Whey–we caals in the troops from Catterick and got them oot. Wad ye believe it? Three weeks later up comes a record on the "Top of the Pops". Ah didn't knaa what the words wez aboot but ah recognised aad Tom's tone of voice when he wez threatenin' them what he wad de with thor plastic geetars".

There is another thing too you should know about. That Geordie gutteral sound is widely used in the film business though credit is never given. Did you see "The Battle of Britain" or "The Longest Day"? You will remember then that the Germans spoke German and it was sub-titled in English. It's long been known in the sound business that coconut shells record better than real horses hoofs when they need a galloping sound. Well it's the same with voices. The producer, knowing well that British cinemagoers don't speak German took a chance which paid off. He employed Joe Cobbles, an old friend of mine, who used to be checkweighman at Hartford Main pit, to do all the voices. You see they found that real German sounded too sweet and sentimental even when they called in ex-Gestapo drill sergeants to do the soundtrack. Even Himmler's second cousin was auditioned and he sounded like Malcolm Muggeridge with a milk flake stuck in his gob. You don't believe me? – go down to Shepherd's Bush studios any Monday morning and you'll see Joe's byke propped up outside the front office. Even Joe's wife recognised his voice and they haven't been speaking to each other for forty years. So – it's up to the native Geordie speakers and you, the new students, to uphold the credit of the ancient languag.

So – Let us begin with a Geordie benediction –
"GANONKIDDA – GITSTUCKIN"

7

TO LEARN GEORDIE
WE BEGIN WITH TYPICAL SOUNDS

This is not such a difficult process as you would think, although those slightly lacking in normal concentration or moral fibre, or possessing an epiglottis of normal proportions, may experience some slight trouble in the first ten years of practice.

The first sound to learn is the Geordie 'R'

This is both rolling and gutteral, combining the best effects of Doctor Finlay at his homeliest with the sound of a very old nanny-goat being sick. Try also to imagine the sort of sound emitted by the late Herr Hitler throwing a tantrum, or even the late Mr. Boris Karloff in his celebrated role as Frankenstein's monster. One could say that it is really an amalgam of all these sounds but not so delicate in timbre.

The sound is very rarely heard outside the Geordie enclave although certain vintage records of Mr. Maurice Chevalier do contain an approximation. The only other race to produce an equivalent of the Geordie 'R' is the Taureg tribe who live just off the motor-way on the Golden Road to Samarkand in an oasis called El-Lishot. Being accustomed to talking through the veils of their burnoosers they have evolved a similar raucous sound. Also, being Moslems, they are not allowed to drink beer and, in consequence, what with all that sand their voices sound quite at home in Geordie territory. A further interesting historical fact about the Geordie 'R' is its subsequent improvement in volume and content in the 19th century. It became an established habit during the Industrial Revolution when hours were long and lunch-breaks short for Geordies to order their second pint of beer while still in the act of consuming their first. This improved the original sound by introducing a gargling note, and resulted in northern barmen being represented in old steel-engravings of the period as dressed in sou'wester and oilskins. All that remains to-day of this traditional costume is the custom of the staff in certain old-fashioned bars in the Geordie heart-lands to wear skin-diving costume and a beer-proof plastic flat cap. Certain enterprising pub

Nineteenth Century Geordie Barman

managers have used this as an excuse to clothe their barmaids in bikinis, quoting local custom in extenuation and causing good-humoured riots.

How to reproduce the original Geordie 'R'

Follow the instructions carefully, keeping this page in front of you so that you may follow the sequence of sounds correctly. Are you ready? Then we'll begin.

Phase One: Open the gob (mouth) to its full extremity.

Phase Two: Keep the gob open and vibrate the tonsils in an anti-clockwise motion producing a gargling sound. Keep the tonsil movement supple and flowing.

Phase Three: Still with the gob open and keeping the tonsils vibrating summon up a hacking cough. Just as this is emerging, change it swiftly into an 'R' sound. Try to think of the sort of 'R' that might emerge from the gob of an asthmatic hyena. (An excellent example may be heard in "The Adventures of Tarzan" episode seventy-three where the monkey hits the hyena over the muzzle with a wrench – a monkey-wrench of course.)

Phase Four: Amalgamate all these sounds into one mighty roar, thus producing the final Geordie 'R' sound in all its pure beauty.

Special Note—

An embrocation compounded of equal parts of surgical spirit and Madras Curry Powder (extra hot) may be used to anoint the tonsils prior to Phase Three. This is a great help to those who live south of the Trent, have been to public school, Sandhurst or work for the B.B.C. and have in consequence a tendency to use 'W'

instead of 'R'. This embrocation is miraculous in effect. As soon as it is applied to the tonsils the recipient immediately shrieks "R"! very loudly.

Very Special Note—

In practising the Geordie 'R' for the first time readers are recommended to wear a truss or similar supporting device.

Check your results

Have you done this? Good. You will easily know if you have pronounced the Geordie 'Ŗ' properly by simple observation. This page will be soaked in saliva. Practice makes perfect, remember. You won't make it but practise anyway – unless of course you are a Taureg tourist from the oasis of El-Lishot.

Now for the second sound:

The Diphthong

The Diphthong is defined as the result of the combination of two adjacent vowels or vowel-like sounds and further described by Professor Jollop of Newcastle University as a 'right load of cobblers'.

It is a split sound, one flowing into another. Students are advised to buy a second-hand trombone and "muck aboot" (experiment) by blowing a gentle raspberry down the mouthpiece while manipulating the slide.

Although a Scot, the well-known trombone player Mr. George Chisholm always manages to produce a Geordie diphthong sound in his virtuoso performance of "Colonel Bogey" – but of course Geordies know that the dominion of their tribe extended at one time well into Scotland and in consequence Mr. Chisholm's perfect Geordie tone is doubtless a hereditary memory becoming externalised.

Examples of the diphthong sound

The pronunciation of many alphabet sounds is typical of the Geordie diphthong:-

A – Ayuh; E – Eyuh; H – Ayutch; J – Jayuh; K – Kayuh; O – O-uh; Y – Why-uh, etc.

11

Here are a few sentences to practise containing the diphthong sounds.

1. "Thor not a *byad tyab*"
   In English this means "These cigarettes are really rather good".
2. "Me da's *byad wi'* the *beyor*".
   In English this means "Father is indisposed".
3. "The aad gaffer's a fond *fyeul*.
   In English "The managing director is of doubtful efficiency". (fyeul – a nit, twit or person of low intelligence, the term 'fond' laying a special emphasis on this disability).
4. "A'm gannin' *hyem* to wor lass".
   In English "I must return to the little woman".
   NOTE:- When a Geordie says this do not take it too literally as it is frequently used as an excuse to leave the bar to avoid paying one's round of drinks.

'Hyem' of course means home; 'wor lass', his lawful wedded wife but sometimes this is a union unblessed by the church. The whole phrase is ambiguous in meaning and may imply a restitution of conjugal rights or a mere human Geordie intention of 'thumpin' her lug'. In English this means an exercise of domestic discipline.

Special Note

All phrases like this may be given a particular intimate or authentic colloquial meaning by the addition of the expression – "Yebuggermar".

This does not, at first hearing, sound polite (but then for that matter the entire Geordie language *never* sounds polite). It is actually a friendly, comradely addition, used in the presence of intimates and can be roughly compared to the Japanese polite noise of hissing through the teeth.

Now practise one of these phrases, together with the new addition.

"A'm gannin' hyem to wor lass – yebuggermar".

Don't forget to lay special emphasis on the final 'R' – "YebuggermaR". Make it sound like "YebuggermaRRRR". Don't forget the special ointment too: lavish the surgical spirit and curry powder compound upon the tonsils. If this makes you spit and you feel embarrassed, practise in the privacy of your own room. Take a large bucket in with you too: accidents will happen.

Now you can practise simple Geordie phrases in public

Preliminary warning – make sure your dentures are well glued in place. You can now venture into the Geordie heart-lands although you are warned not to wear either a bowler hat (in Geordie called a 'dut') or a deer stalker cap. The natives may mistake you for an official of the Income Tax department, one of the landed gentry or a Member of Parliament. You may thus be the innocent cause of a rising of the tribes or an international incident. It may even be necessary to extricate you by gunboat or helicopter. Wearing a flat tweed cap may possibly endear you to the natives. This is an example of sartorial and national solidarity, like the fez, the Scottish tam-o-shanter, the Texan sombrero or President Kenyatta's fly-whisk. It is of the same significance too as the Ghandi-cap. Don't, however, wear a yellow waistcoat with it, knickerbockers or a Norfolk jacket, or you may find yourself the subject of an ambush in such areas as Seaham Harbour where the second coming of Lord Londonderry is hourly awaited with sadistic glee. Having taken these precautions you are ready to commence your preliminary safari, although it is *not* recommended that you journey, at this stage, further than Bensham.

Now let us assume that your native guide has led you to the territory of the former head-hunters of Bensham. *Do not be tempted to proceed further to Low Fell,* merely because they are said to speak fluent English there. This territory is continually under siege by neighbouring tribes from Windy Nook who cherish a hatred for renegades who talk humpybacked. In this militant atmosphere the drums of the Windy Nookers thud all night as the tribesmen mass for the assault and the Low Fellers keep up their spirits by singing their National Anthem "The working clarss can kiss my foot, I've got the foreman's job at larrst". It is also whispered that the Low Fellers are obsessed with SEX. They insist that their coal or domestic fuel be delivered at all times in such receptacles.

Waiting for Lord Londonderry

14

"Weor's the netty?

Now we are ready to converse with the natives

Approach the hostelry (known to the natives as a "Boozah") confidently push open the bar door and address the nearest barman in the following terms:-

"Gizabroonjack"

In English this means "Good evening potman, kindly pour me a pint of brown ale."

Brown ale is of course the wine of the country although there is quite a large faction (the "Klubganner" tribe) who pay allegiance to the beverage known as "Fed".

You can, if you wish, instil confidence in your audience (for by now you will have one) by spitting on the floor, or, if in the sitting-room rather than the bar, by spitting in the fire. Check first that it is not an electric fire as this may cause a power cut. Having obtained the beverage, hold firmly on to your temples and drink it. Once the ale is drunk there is a further phrase which you will find necessary.

"Weor's the netty?"

In English this means "Can you direct me to the men's room?"

After you have thrown up – don't be ashamed, because any fool who tries to drink their first brown ale in one gulp always does this. The few who don't have a coronary.

You may now relax and it will be expected that you join in the conversation. A good opening gambit is

"Hoositganninathematch?"

In English this means "How is the football game progressing". Do not be afraid to ask this because there is always a football match going on somewhere in the tribal reservation. If the local home team is seven goals down or even playing a draw, one of their supporters will doubtless remark:

"Thebuggarswantshingin' "

In English this means "I have the gravest doubts as to the ability of the directors of the football team". If however the team is winning or merely avoiding relegation successfully, they will say:

"Thordeeincanny"

In English this means "Our noble lads are performing successfully with their usual skill".

By now the brown ale will doubtless have gone to your head and you will be filled with gas and boundless confidence. However, do not be tempted into too ambitious a conversation. Whatever is said, whether you understand or not (and you won't) it will suffice to mutter at symmetrical spaces in the conversation:

"Whyaye"

(meaning: "I absolutely agree old chap" or alternatively "I find your conversation stimulating". In fact it is perfectly possible to conduct a four hour conversation by alternately grunting or saying "Whyaye" (pronounced WHY-IY). To avoid too much monosyllabic comment you can of course add the magic additive phrase you learned before. Rember it? Of course you do:

"Yebuggermar"

Now link these two alternatives:

"Whyaye yebuggermar" or

"(Grunt) yebuggermar".

Shortly the barman will genuflect and utter the final benediction:

"Seeyordrinksofflads" (In English "Time gentlemen please").

Now, your first safari safely over you can gan hyem to yor lass and vomit in comfort in the privacy of your hotel netty. See how you have already learned the idiom?

"Seeyordrinksofflads!"

17

The next morning you will feel horrible

You must however go back to the same "boozah" so that you do not lose your confidence. This is in pursuance of the old Geordie folk-legend which is spoken thus:

"Watmadeyabad 'll makeyabettor"

You won't have the strength to add "Yebuggermar". But 'nil desperandum', at least you can spread light among the regular customers and improve your relations with them by declaiming as you enter the 'boozah':

"Fillthubar"

This will cause consternation and you will discover that fresh customers have miraculously appeared from nowhere.

NOTE:

In English, the first phrase implies that more brown ale will overcome the nausea of the initial dose. The second phrase indicates that it didn't bo her you at all and you wish to demonstrate the fact publicly by buying beer for all. This will, be warned, cost you a small fortune, but it's ten to one that wherever you come from the rate of exchange will be in your favour. Besides that you will be the talk of the neighbourhood for many years and may even become the subject of a folk-tale handed down from father to son. Imagine your delight if your son or grandson were to visit the reservation and be greeted. thus by the descendants of your co-drinkers:

"Yuwadn'tbekin te the fondfyeul that bowtbeer for the lads?"

This is the opening stanza of the ballad which praises your name and remembers your charitable works.

A special note about "Broon"

Although every Geordie knows about "Broon" you may sometimes hear them speak of it in other terms.

Term One: "Lunatics' broth" – the term is self-explanatory. All Geordies will claim that *their* local hospital has a special drying-out ward for "broon" drinkers. This is not quite correct. In point of fact, it is really not a "broon" *ward* but a special "broon" *mortuary*.

Term Two: "Jawney inter spayus" – named after a famous steam radio programme in English called "Journey into Space". Again, self-explanatory.

Let us visit the Geordie in his native wigwam

There are many sub-tribes in Geordie-land. Some have deserted the ways of their forefathers, become urbanised and live in semi-detached houses. We can find little of tradition among these renegades as they all speak a debased form of English known as "High West Jesmond" or "Darras Hall". The latter live in a fortified enclave to the north of Newcastle, the women-folk, so the natives maintain, wearing fur coats and "ne-knickers". This original statement has been found to be untrue due to a natural mistake in translation. It should really be knee-knickers, these being necessary due to the fact that many of the older bungalows have "ootside netties", and the winds in those parts blow cold.

An old native who recently visited his son-in-law there stated to me:
" 'Sennuftoblaayerlugsofftheor"
thus endorsing the windy nature of the enclave.

Then we have the semi-urbanised inhabitants who live in larger terrace houses. Many of these are students who commute only between each other's pads and the bun room at the University. Most of them are regrettably foreigners really, from as far south as the Home Counties. Many of these have never even seen a native Geordie and imagine that they talk like Jimmy Saville or Ena Sharples. The Geordie native tolerates these poor migrants in spite of the fact that he firmly believes that they spend their entire university life growing their hair, taking trips and digging up cricket pitches. The students, for their part, imagine that the natives spend their lives growing enormous leeks and beating their wives, which is not completely true.

Then we have the smaller-wigwam Geordies who are now mostly emigrating to multi-storey wigwams. These are probably the most civilised of all – due to insufficient sound-proofing they have had to stop beating their wives altogether. A further contributory reason is that due to the inefficiency of the lifts, the male Geordie is too exhausted to even think of beating his wife. Not like the old days when it was lift the sneck on the back door and belt 'yor lass' as soon as you got in. Then we have the "cooncil hoose" Geordies. These, too, have stopped beating their wives

because the "cooncil estates" are so far from their place of work
that they have barely time to assert their conjugal rights before its
time to get up for work again. The women-folk are extremely
moral because it's so far to walk to the shops that the cold winds
kill the inclination. We are left with the most powerful and primitive inheritors of the traditions of the Geordie nation: the
"Pitmatic" Geordies or "Yackers". These live often in very long
rows of low wigwams. In the back street, set in the centre, are
smaller subsidiary wigwams called "netties". For some reason
no-one ever uses the front entrance to the main wigwam except
for the usual tribal ceremonies connected with birth, death or
marriage. Consequently there is long grass in the front street and
mud in the back, since street-paving is looked upon as a softening
luxury even by the National Coal Board.

Another strange custom is that of never numbering the back doors and as the front is either nailed up or you can't see it for grass it is easy to get lost. The natives have their own method of identification – a local chief told me recently, "it's easy ter find wor hoose, sivin netties past the rain barrel".

Now you have been introduced to the natives, let us hear their language at home

We will begin with a typical morning dialogue. Mother is grilling an enormous leek for breakfast, father is still asleep. The time is 7.15 a.m. The traditional method of waking father (or "da", generally qualified as "wor da") is to shout twice. One to initially shake him from his usual "broon ale" stupor, the second to encourage him to wash, shave and descend to eat the enormous leek. Hence the dialogue goes like this:-

Wor Muther:	"Y'up"?	time 7.15 a.m.
Wor da:	"A'mup!"	time 7.16 a.m.
Wor Muther:	"Y'upyit?"	time 7.20 a.m.
Wor da:	"A'mupnoo!"	time 7.21 a.m.

Seeing that the men-folk work long shifts and go out to the 'club' each night while the womenfolk stay in and make 'proggy mats' there is little further conversation to report. By the time "wor da" has come back from the club, checked the barbed wire round the leek bed, fed the leeks with pigs' blood and aspirins, taken the whippet for a walk and wound his watch, it is time for a short nap and then resume the morning traditional greetings. Remember them?

That's right. "Y'up?" "A'mupnoo!"

And so life goes on in Foreman's Row while the buzzer blows at the 'Bella pit, and the cursing colliers count the days to redundancy. As you have seen there is little to teach you in the way of conversation at this point, the primitive Geordies very rarely speaking more than one word at a time. Even when they speak sixteen words it still sounds like one. Therefore a list of words, a vocabulary, will follow.

Before the vocabulary a short exercise. Let us translate a poem. The author of this has never been traced and as it is also out of copyright it stands in imminent danger of being set to music by Lionel Bart. Several authorities have searched diligently for the man who wrote it, including Jon Silkin, Basil Bunting, Dan Smith, Arthur Grey and Uncle Tom Pickard and all. The Northern Arts Association have also offered a reward of 14 pesetas, 26 zlotys, 4 old francs and a rupee, being the contents of the pockets of the lead jews-harp performer of the Northern Sinfonia when he got back from their last tour. The poem is magnificently minimal and goes something like this:

> There wes an aad wife o' Byker
> There wes an aad wife o' Byker
> She up with the pan,
> And flattened her man,
> There wes an aad wife o' Byker.

Now the translation.

"In the medieval township and bailiewick of Byker there dwelt an aged crone. Suspecting her spouse of infidelity she apprehended him "in flagrante delicto" consorting with a young female of doubtful repute from the neighbouring lordship of Heaton. As he rose from the grass of Heaton Park adjusting his clothing before leaving in accordance with the municipal notice displayed in the park convenience, she clove him to the gizzard with a non-stick frying pan and was condemned at the next Assizes."

Can anything demonstrate better the magnificent economy of the Geordie language? So few words in the original – so many in the translation!

Now we have some prose and it is your turn to translate:

The first exercise is a monologue about a man called Ned Wright, a leading character in a Gateshead factory called Hawks. It was (ne kiddin' kidder) written by a man called John Atlantic Stephenson in the 19th century. There are many variations – here is one:

Haaks's Men

Aah fell in the other day wi' Ned Wright. Ye knaa Ned and four and twenty o' Haaks's men went oot t' the war agyen the French te de a favour fer the Duke o' Wellinton. ("Did ye knaa the Duke?" ah axes him. "Did aa knaa the Duke" sez Ned, "him and me was weel aquent, he caalled me Ned and ah caalled him Nosey".) Well Ned and the lads is hevvin' a gill when ower cums the Duke. "Watcheer Ned" sez Wellinton. "Whatfettle the day Nosey?" sez Ned. "Aa've got a job fer ye and yor lads" sez the Duke. "Fer ye Nosey" sez Ned, "it's deun already". ("Him and we wez marras", sez Ned). Onyway he taps Ned up to shift a regiment av the French what was workin' themselves a pennorth on top of a hill. "Ye see them sowljers on the top o' thon hill thonder" sez the Duke. "Ah want thim shifted; not just josselled – ah want thim shifted aaltegither." "Man hinny", sez Ned, "it's ne bother at aal". (Me and Nosey wez aad marras, sez Ned). So he calls up Bob Robson, the dabbest hand at coontin' ye iver saa. "Bob" he sez, "Hoo many men on the top o' thon hill thonder?" "Fower hundred" sez Bob deed quick. "Hoo many men div ye

23

want te shift them?" sez the Duke. "Aall tek twenty" sez Ned. "Man there's fower hundred" sez Nosey. "Aalreet" sez Ned, "Divn't get yer bowels in an uproar – aal tyek twenty-fower te be on the safe side". So off gans Ned with fower and twenty o' Haaks's men – tappy lappy doon the lonnen when roond the corner comes Napoleon on a bonny white cuddy. "What gans on, Ned?" sez Napoleon. "We're off to shift them sowljers o' yours" sez Ned. "Whey man, ye canna de that Ned – them's me crack regiment". "Cum bye" said Ned, "Nosey sez they gan and gan they will". But Napoleon lashes up his bonny white cuddy and rides it hetfoot up the fell, shootin' "Gan back ye fond fyeuls – it's Ned Wright and four and twenty o' Haaks's men – ye hevn't a happorth o' chance". Man ye couldnt' see them for a clood o' clarts and the battle o' Waterloo wez ower. ("Did aa knaa Wellinton, why man aa would think shyem" sez Ned.)

Now translate this into Queen's English. Use the vocabulary at the back of the book.

Now another exercise.

The Old Testament is said to have been translated by the Venerable Bede especially for the Jarrow lads. You will recall he kept a monastery just round the back of the Slake near the oil tanks opposite Geordie Palmer's allotment.

The original manuscript read as follows, written as it was in pure archaic Geordie.

It comes from the Book of Exodus.

"Noo the gaffer ov aal the Israelites was a chep caalled Moses and he fell oot wi' Pharaoh whe wez the gaffer ov aal the Egyptians. So Moses sez to his lads, "Howway ower the Reed Sea." So they aall set oot wi' thor bairns and thor posstubs, whippets and galloways te plodge ower the watter. "Had on" sez Moses, "Had on". And he hoisted his deppity's stick up ahight. Whey man ye wadn't credit it. The watters parted. Thor wez a waall o' water on one side and a waall o' watter on the other. So thor wez ne caall to plodge ower. So off sets the Israelites ahint Moses and eftei them, het-foot across the scaadin' het sands comes Pharaoh and his lads. "Hey up" sez Pharaoh "noo we've got them", and he gets his lads te whip up thor cuddies and they sets off te bray the Israelites – het foot across the scaadin' het sands – tappy lappy ower the bed o' the Reed Sea. Thor wez a waal o' watter on one side and a waal o' watter on t'other. They wor gannin' like the clappers – cuddies, brakes and sowljers – and man thor wor just aboot te bray the poor Israelites when Moses torns roond. He up wi' 'is deppity's stick hoyin' it reet up ahight. What a gan on – doon cum the waall o' watter on one side – doon cum the waall o' watter on t'other and ivery last bugger of the Egyptians wez drooned forbye the smallest one, young Ahmed, and he got his wellies stuck in the clarts."

Translate this exercise into the Queen's English. Bearing in mind the present situation in the Middle East – try to avoid giving offence to either Egypt or Israel as we Geordies are officially neutral. But don't worry too much; whatever solution you arrive at you're going to get hell from Enoch Powell anyway.

Finally, one last exercise, a short one from the New Testament. This was written for the Epilogue on Tyne Tees Television but as all the staff were said to be either Londoners or Australians it was impossible to find anyone capable of reading it correctly.

The Prodigal Son

Thor wez this rich bookie and he had a son. By, he wez a bad 'un, aalways gannin' roond the clubs – 'e'd even been hoyed oot the Dolce Vita and he wez barred from Bower's Restaurant. So 'e ups and leaves hyem an' tyeks a flat in Osborne Road. It wezn't lang before he gets hoyed oot o' there fer distorbin' the students by havin' wild parties thro the day and the Squad wez eftor him for tekin' trips on Capstan Full Strength. What a worky ticket he wez. Finally he falls on bad times and gans from bad te worse. He'd tried everythin'. He gans oot on the hot-dog barrers but got the sack for watterin' doon the mustard, and finally gits right doon on his beam ends workin' in the Ministry at Benton. One day his fethor's hevin' a gill wi the' lads in the Gosforth Park Hotel when in staggers the poor prodigal lad. The doorman had let him in thinkin' he wez an eccentric millionaire. There 'e stud, poor lad, thin as a rake without a byeut to 'is foot and his britches backside hingin' oot. His fethor torned aroond and when he saw his poor prodigal son, what d'ye think he did? He caalled the doorman and had him hoyed oot.

This pitiful tale, bristling with morals, should prove a fine exercise.

And now – to the vocabulary.

VOCABULARY OF GEORDIE PHRASES

These are not arranged alphabetically but under subject headings.   G for Geordie,   E for English.

SPORT (Football)

G.	Morderthebee	E.	We disagree with the referee's decision.
G.	Massacree thim	E.	Play up, play up, and play the game.
G.	Dunsh 'im	E.	Tackle your opponent.
G.	Givower dunshin	E.	Kindly do not push, the ground is very congested.
G.	Yewantipackin	E.	Apply for a transfʌr.
G.	Worbairncan de bettor	E.	Your tactics are at fault.

There are many more expressions which will be published later under a plain cover. Adults only. State your profession and age.

LEISURE

G.	Ah wes palatick	E.	I enjoyed myself.
G.	Ah scoredwithabord	E.	I made the acquaintance of a young woman.
G.	Howay doon to the Chinese, pet.	E.	Would you care to dine with me?
G.	Gantethehop?	E.	Are you attending the Young Conservatives Ball?
G.	Fancyadance?	E.	May I have the last waltz?
G.	Givower ahmsweatin'	E.	No thank you.
G.	Ahfancyhor or Ahfancyhim	E.	Can this be love at first sight?

27

G.	Mindshesweelstacked	E.	What a stunning figure that young lady has.
G.	Hey Sparrasankles	E.	Excuse me miss.
G.	Areyeworkin yersel?	E.	I trust you are not trying to provoke a disturbance.
G.	Ootside!	E.	Let us settle this matter in a civilised manner.
G.	Yeandme	E.	Man to man like gentlemen.
G.	Gizashort	E.	A small whisky, or May I have a shirt?
G.	Seymagen kidder	E.	Would you repeat the order waiter?
G.	Broonsalroond	E.	Brown ales for my friends landlord/potman/waiter.
G.	The tyebl's claggy	E.	Waiter, could you bring a cloth as the table is awash with beer.
G.	Divvent drop ye dottle on the proggy mat	E.	(Generally spoken by landlords and waiters). Please do not drop hot ash on the carpet.

AT THE RESTAURANT

G.	Gissies tetties and bagies	E.	I wish to order pork, potatoes and a little turnip, please.
G.	Yerboodies clarty	E.	The plate is dusty.
G.	Yer fadge is ower femmer	E.	The bread is too crumbly.
G.	The polony's foisty	E.	The salami seems to be mouldy
G.	Gizthemeatantetties	E.	I think I would prefer the meat and potatoes.
G.	Mindyorkiddin'	E.	You have miscalculated the bill.
G.	Smashinbaitthat	E.	I enjoyed the meal.
G.	Weezonthebar?	E.	Can you call the wine waiter?

G. Doonthehatch	E. Jolly good health chaps.
G. It gansin and ganzoot, taak aboot hoyin' munny away.	E. A polite friendly remark suitable for the men's room.

THE HOME

G. Wordaz on the buroo	E. Father is unemployed.
G. Agorrit on a storeclub	E. It was obtained on credit at the Co-operative Wholesale Society.
G. Eez away te the dole for 'is munny.	E. Father is out on an errand.
G. Givower bubblin' or aal dad yer jaa	E. Cease your grizzling, child, or I will punish you.
G. Hadaway an' get a shyeul o' coal oot the cree.	E. Put some coal on the fire, please.
G. Ye've left yer bogey in the yard	E. Tut, tut, child; you have not put your kiddy-car away.
G. Giz a bullet	E. May I have one of your sweetmeats?
G. The chimlas ahad.	E. The chimney has caught fire.
G. Gan on coin yer gord	E. Let me see you turn your hoop in a circle, Felicity.
G. Yerbyeuts is clarty	E. Your boots are muddied.
G. Yerg'annies cowped her creels	E. Your grandmother has stumbled.
G. Aal cloot yer lugs	E. I am sorry but corporal punishment appears necessary.
G. Me da's in a fine fettle	E. Father is in good spirits.
G. Mind them's bonny galluses	E. I say, I do admire your taste in braces.
G. Worbairn's hacky mucky.	E. The baby needs a wash.
G. Wor Geordie's gannin strights.	E. My son George is betrothed.
G. Why aye hinny.	E. Certainly darling.

PUBLIC TRANSPORT

G. Hoy – ye
E. Taxi!

G. Giztwofives
E. Two to Byker Bridge please.

G. Nipyortab doonstairs
E. Smoking is not permitted on the lower deck.

G. Dyer gan b'the Fower Lane ends?
E. Does this bus go to Benton.

G. Lowp oot fer the Central
E. Will all passengers for Newcastle Central Station kindly alight?

G. Aall oot fer the hoppins
E. Will all passengers for the Temperance Festival on Newcastle Town Moor please alight.

G. The bus is lorchin like a shuggyboat.
E. This bus is very unsteady.

G. Say taa taa te yor da
E. Wave father farewell.

THE CLUB

G. Fowerfedz
E. Four Federation ales please.

G. Gizyersubs
E. Have you paid your club dues?

G. Bestuvordernoo
E. Pray silence gentlemen.

G. Areyegannagiz the bestuvorder?
E. May I insist on silence!

G. Bestuvorderorootyegan
E. Shut up or get out.

G. Eyesdoon luk in
E. The bingo game is commencing

G. Letshevyordrinks off
E. The licence does not permit us to serve more drinks.

G. Onesinger onesong noo
E. Kindly do not compete with the artiste.

G. Haad yer gobs fer Geordie
E. Pray silence for the concert chairman.

G. Duts off fer the Queen
E. Remove your headgear when the National Anthem is played

G. We's buggered the bandit
E. It appears that someone has broken the fruit machine.

30

For a simple and short dictionary of Geordie dialect today the reader will find Todd's *Geordie Words and Phrases* the best introduction.

GEORDIE WORDS AND PHRASES by George Todd. An aid to communication on Tyneside and thereabouts. 48 Pages of useful phrases, such as —

blaan-oot
Aa'm fair blaan-oot

blown-out
I have eaten too much food

howk
Divvint howk yor sneck

pick: dig
Do not pick your nose

kyek
Gi's a bit o' kyek

cake
Give me a piece of cake

. . . and many others

ISBN 0 946928 09 6

THE NEW GEORDIE DICTIONARY
edited by Frank Graham.

There is no definitive Geordie dialect. There are considerable variations in the speech spoken in Northumberland and Durham, partly geographical changing from north to south, partly occupational as illustrated by the mining and farming communities. The urban areas, particularly Tyneside, have also developed words and phrases with different meanings from those used in rural districts.

This dictionary uses the word *Geordie* in a very loose and general sense. 48 Pages and many hundred entries.

ISBN 0 946928 11 8